REPTILES

Jen Green

Belitha Press

LOOK FOR THE GECKO

Look for the gecko in boxes like this. Here you will find extra facts, stories and other interesting information about reptiles.

Produced by
Monkey Puzzle Media Ltd.,
Gissing's Farm, Fressingfield,
Suffolk IP21 5SH, UK

First published in the UK in 2002 by
Belitha Press Limited
An imprint of Chrysalis Books plc,
64 Brewery Road,
London N7 9NT, UK

Designer: Tim Mayer
Editor: Sarah Doughty
Consultant: Joyce Pope

ISBN 1 84138 362 7

British Library Cataloguing in Publication Data for this book is available from the British Library.

Printed in Hong Kong
10 9 8 7 6 5 4 3 2 1

Acknowledgements
We wish to thank the following individuals and organizations for their help and assistance and for supplying material in their collections: Bruce Coleman Collection 13 top (Alain Compost), 22 bottom, 30 (Robert Maier); Corbis front cover (Gallo Images/Anthony Bannister), 1 (Michael & Patricia Fogden), 2 (Paul A Souders), 3 (Roger De La Harpe), 4 (Charles & Josette Lenars), 5 bottom (Michael & Patricia Fogden), 6 top (Kevin Schafer), 6-7 (Stephen Frink), 7 top (David A Northcott), 8 (Paul A Souders), 9 bottom (Gallo Images /Anthony Bannister), 13 bottom (Gallo Images), 15 (Michael & Patricia Fogden), 16 top (Yann Arthus-Bertrand), 16 bottom (David A Northcott), 18 (David A Northcott), 19 bottom (Mary Ann McDonald), 20 bottom (Michael & Patricia Fogden), 21 (Kevin Schafer), 22 top (David A Northcott), 23 (Gallo Images/Roger De La Harpe), 24 left (Michael S Yamashita), 24 right (Wolfgang Kaehler), 25 (Charles & Josette Lenars), 26 (David A Northcott), 27 (Stuart Westmorland), 28 (Gallo Images/Anthony Bannister), 29 (Lynda Richardson); Digital Vision back cover top, back cover bottom left, 11 top; NHPA back cover bottom right (Stephen Dalton), 10 (Stephen Dalton), 11 bottom (Stephen Dalton), 12 (Martin Harvey), 14 (Stephen Dalton), 19 top (Image Quest 3-D), 20 top (Martin Harvey), 31 (Robert Erwin); Oxford Scientific Films 5 top (John Mitchell), 17 (Frank Schneidermeyer); Science Photo Library 9 top (DT Roberts).

▼ The thorny devil is just one of the many weird reptiles in this book. Turn to page 8 to find out more.

▶ A crocodile carries her young into the water for the first time. Turn to page 23 for more reptile parents.

CONTENTS

THE WEIRD WORLD OF REPTILES

Which group of animals are the weirdest and scariest on Earth? For many people the answer would be reptiles. The reptile family includes small, darting lizards, slithery snakes and hard-shelled tortoises. Giant crocodiles with rows of sharp teeth are reptiles too.

Reptiles are one of the Earth's main groups of animals. The dinosaurs, which lived on the planet millions of years ago, were also reptiles, but they died out long ago.

Today there are about 6500 different species, or kinds, of reptiles. The reptile family can be divided into four main groups: snakes, lizards, turtles and crocodiles. Over half of all living reptiles are lizards. Most of the rest are snakes.

◀ Lizards are the largest family of reptiles. Chameleons, geckos, iguanas (shown here) and skinks are all types of lizard too.

4

REPTILE EGGS

Most reptiles bury their eggs in the soil. The babies growing inside are protected by the egg's tough shell. When fully grown, the young reptiles break out of their shells. This is called hatching.

◀ Snakes are reptiles with long, thin bodies and no legs. This group of reptiles includes cobras, vipers and boas, such as the emerald boa shown here.

Reptiles vary a lot in size and shape, but they also have many things in common. For example, all reptiles have a scaly skin. Scales are small, hard layers of skin that overlap and cover the body of the reptile. Scales help to protect it from enemies. Many reptiles produce young by laying eggs but some produce live young.

▶ Crocodiles are a group of large, fierce reptiles. This group includes alligators, caimans and gharials (like this one).

REPTILES EVERYWHERE

▲ Tuataras are very rare. They live only on a few small islands around New Zealand.

WHAT'S IN A NAME?

Tuataras look like lizards but have a spiny crest running down their backs. The Maori people of New Zealand gave these strange reptiles their name, which means 'peaks on the back'.

Reptiles live in many different places – on dry land, in lakes, rivers or the sea. Reptiles don't live in very cold places such as the Arctic. They need heat from the sun to keep them warm.

The thick, leafy forests around the Equator are home to many different reptiles. Others are found in cooler woodlands and in grasslands. Some reptiles, such as geckos, even share our homes. Deserts can be harsh places where very little rain falls and the sun shines down fiercely.

You may be surprised to learn that many kinds of reptiles, including snakes, lizards and tortoises, live in deserts.

Many reptiles spend their lives in or around fresh or salt water. Crocodiles live in swamps or rivers. Turtles and terrapins live in lakes and streams. Sea turtles swim in the open ocean.

Worm-lizards are a weird group of reptiles that spend their lives burrowing underground. They are neither worms nor lizards. There are 140 different kinds of these strange creatures! Most have no legs.

▲ Desert reptiles like this desert tortoise spend the hottest part of the day hiding under stones or sheltering in cool burrows.

◀ Marine iguanas are lizards that live on rocky seashores. They dive off rocks to feed on seaweed under the water.

Cold Blood and Scaly Skins

Reptiles have a bony skeleton like we do. Like us, they also have a brain, heart, lungs and a stomach and intestines to digest food.

Reptiles come in many different shapes and sizes. Turtles have an unusual shape: their shell is part of their skeleton. Snakes and some lizards are different from other reptiles too: they have no legs. But most reptiles have a long, slim body and a tail, with four short legs that spread sideways to take their weight.

A reptile's scales are made of a tough material called keratin. Your fingernails are made of the same stuff. The scales form a barrier like a suit of armour. But unlike armour, the reptile's skin is bendy, so it can move about.

All reptiles shed or lose their old scales from time to time. This is called moulting.

▼ Some reptiles have extra armour. The thorny devil is a lizard with sharp spikes on its body to keep enemies away.

▲ The scales on the skin of this temple viper protect it from enemies yet allow it to move freely.

▼ This snake is shedding its skin. Its empty skin looks like a ghost snake!

Underneath is a new scaly skin. Most reptiles shed their scales either one at a time or in patches. Snakes shed their skin in one piece.

All reptiles are 'cold-blooded'. This doesn't mean they are always cold. Unlike us, they need the sun's heat energy to warm their muscles so they can move around. They change their body temperature by moving between warm and cool places throughout the day.

ACTION STATIONS!

Tortoises are famous for moving very slowly. Most other types of reptiles can zip about fast. Some are expert swimmers, others are skillful climbers. A few lizards and snakes can even glide through the air!

Lizards are speedy runners. They scurry quickly over the ground, swinging their bodies from side to side to take long strides. Chameleons scramble about in trees with the help of rough soles on their feet, which help them to grip smooth branches. Tree snakes have ridged scales on their bellies that work in the same way.

◀ A chameleon's toes have scaly soles with tiny hairs that grip like clingfilm. They grip so well that the lizard can climb sheer walls and even run across the ceiling upside-down!

SLITHERY BUT SPEEDY

Some snakes are fast movers, even though they have no legs. Snakes move in different ways. Some bunch their body into tight coils and then straighten it out again, in a concertina-style movement against the ground. Others, such as sidewinders, throw their bodies into S-shaped curves which press against the ground.

▶ A tree snake slithers among the leaves and branches of a tree.

Some reptiles are strong swimmers. Crocodiles zoom through the water by thrashing their strong tails from side to side. Tortoises are slow on land, but sea turtles are fast swimmers. They flap their front flippers up and down underwater like birds flap their wings in the air.

No reptile can fly, but lizards called flying dragons can glide through the air by spreading flaps of loose skin on their sides. The flaps act like a parachute, so the reptile can glide down from the treetops to the ground.

▼ The basilisk lizard can run across the surface of a pool to escape from its enemies. Sheer speed keeps it afloat, and its long tail helps it to balance.

SUPER SENSES

Reptiles find out about the world around them by using their senses – sight, hearing, smell, taste and touch. Some reptiles have extra-special senses to help them find food or escape enemies quickly.

Snakes don't have eardrums, so they can't hear in the same way we do. Snakes have sensitive skin and bones which help them to feel vibrations (small movements) in the ground. They can sense when other animals are approaching even when they cannot see or hear them.

▼ A crocodile's eyes and nostrils are set high on its head. It can see and smell while most of its body is hidden underwater.

Snakes and some lizards can actually taste smells! They flick their forked tongues in and out to collect tiny amounts of smells in the air or on the ground. Then they put their tongue to a sensitive patch on the roof of their mouth or around the mouth to identify the smells. This patch is called the Jacobson's organ.

▶ Snakes, such as this tree snake from Java, gather scents from the air with their tongues.

▼ Chameleons can move their eyes in different directions. This means they can hunt for food in two different areas.

Snakes' eyes are always open – they can't even blink. Their eyes are covered by see-through scales which keep dust out. Some lizards have very large eyes that help them see in the dark. Many snakes, including boas, have a super-sense which they use for hunting – they can see heat. A boa has special patches on its lips which help the snake see the body heat of warm animals such as birds, bats and mice. The boa uses this sense to hunt, even in the dead of night.

A THIRD EYE

Tuataras and some lizards have a 'third eye' on top of their heads. This weird, skin-covered patch senses light and dark. Experts think it helps these reptiles to adjust to life in the different seasons, with changing daylight hours.

FIERCE HUNTERS

Most reptiles are carnivores (meat-eaters). Smaller species mainly hunt insects, worms, shellfish, mice – and other reptiles. Very large snakes and crocodiles have been known to hunt animals as big as deer and buffalo.

Caimans, alligators and crocodiles are clever hunters. They lie in wait in waterholes and rivers, and pounce on animals coming to the water's edge to drink. The crocodile lunges forward with a splash, grabs its prey and sinks back underwater.

▼ A chameleon shoots out its long, sticky tongue to catch insect food.

Snakes have special hinged jaws that can open very wide. They can swallow creatures larger than their own heads!

LESS FOOD

Cold-blooded reptiles do not need to make heat for their bodies from the food they eat. They keep warm by lying in the sun. This means that they need a lot less food than warm-blooded animals such as humans. Some reptiles only eat three or four meals a year!

Tortoises move too slowly to catch animal food, so they are mainly plant-eaters. But, the alligator snapping turtle, who lives in streams and rivers, is a meat-eating hunter. This turtle has a slim, pink tongue that looks like a wriggling worm. It opens its mouth to attract small fish. When the fish swims in, hoping to catch the 'worm', the turtle catches the fish instead! It snaps up the fish in its strong jaws.

Snakes called constrictors kill their prey by squeezing them to death. They wrap their bodies around an animal so tightly that it cannot breathe in, so it dies from lack of air. Snakes cannot chew or bite so they simply swallow their food whole.

DEADLY WEAPONS

Reptiles can be dangerous creatures. Many crocodiles are powerful enough to kill humans. Some snakes and a few lizards are armed with deadly poison. They use the poison to kill their prey and to defend themselves.

▲ Open wide! A fully grown crocodile has more than 60 sharp teeth.

But most snakes aren't poisonous. Only a few have venom (poison) strong enough to harm humans. People are sometimes bitten by snakes which they tread on accidentally. Medicine called anti-venom is used to treat snake bites.

A crocodile's main weapons are its sharp teeth. Unlike human teeth, a crocodile's teeth never stop growing. Throughout its life, old, worn-out teeth drop out and are replaced by new, sharp ones.

▲ The gila monster is one of only two types of poisonous lizard. Both live in the deserts of southern USA and Mexico.

▶ A snake's venom is made in two glands in its head. The venom trickles down grooved channels in the snake's long, curved teeth, known as fangs. When the snake bites, the poison is injected into its prey.

SWINGING FANGS

Most snakes have fangs which are fixed in their mouths like ordinary teeth. But rattlesnakes and vipers have fangs on hinges. The fangs are usually folded back, but swing forward into the biting position as the snake strikes at its prey.

ESCAPE ARTISTS

Reptiles face many dangers. Birds, mammals, spiders and larger reptiles all try to eat them. Some species have developed clever tricks to avoid being harmed.

Lizards are top of the menu for many hungry hunters. Most lizards escape from danger by scurrying away as fast as they can! Frilled lizards use a special trick to put off predators. They have loose skin around their neck which they can raise to make themselves look scary. The lizard also hisses loudly, lashes its tail and frightens away its enemy! The frill also makes the lizard more difficult to swallow if an enemy attacks.

◄ The frilled lizard raises the skin around its neck to look like a much larger animal.

Turtles and tortoises have built-in armour – a hard shell which protects their back and belly. Most can draw their head and neck right inside their shell. The stinkpot turtle has an extra weapon. When threatened, it gives off a horrible stink!

Some clever lizards can shed their own tail to escape attackers. If a hungry predator attacks the lizard, its tail breaks off. The attacker is distracted by the tail wriggling on the ground and the lizard can make a quick getaway!

▲ The wonder gecko's tail breaks off at a special point. In time, the tail grows back again.

▲ When they are threatened, some horned lizards can shoot a thin jet of blood from their eyes to put off an attacker.

PLAYING DEAD

Some snakes play dead if danger threatens. Harmless grass snakes roll on their backs if an enemy approaches. The snake lies quite still with its mouth open and its tongue hanging out. When the enemy has gone, the snake 'comes to life' again.

CLEVER COLOURS

▲ In the deserts of Australia, the skink's bright blue tongue may help it to avoid becoming a predator's next meal.

Many reptiles avoid their enemies by blending in well with their surroundings. These natural disguises are called camouflage. There are some weird and wonderful disguises in the reptile world! Other reptiles use very bright colours to stand out from their surroundings and surprise other animals.

Chameleons use camouflage very cleverly. They can change their body colour from green to brown or black, so they blend in with different backgrounds as they move about.

American horned lizards with sharp spines along their bodies and pointed horns on the top of their heads look frightening. However, they are quite harmless. They depend on camouflage skills to help them blend in with their desert homes and avoid their enemies.

▼ Could you tell a poisonous coral snake (below) from a harmless milk snake which has similar colours?

KEEP AWAY!

Warning colours are used by many different types of animals, not just reptiles. Poisonous fish and stinging insects such as wasps also have bright stripes or spots on their bodies that keep enemies away.

Some reptiles use bright colours to surprise an attacker. The blue-tongued skink is a sandy-coloured lizard. If cornered by an enemy, it opens its mouth wide to display its bright blue tongue. The startled enemy may hesitate for a second – buying the lizard precious seconds to scurry away.

Poisonous coral snakes have bright red, yellow and black striped markings. These colours act as a warning, telling predators that the snake is poisonous. Milk snakes are not poisonous, but have very similar markings. Predators are fooled and leave the milk snake alone.

▶ **The chameleon's skin contains grains of different colours. These grains can be spread out or clumped together to create different colours and shapes depending on the surroundings.**

BABY REPTILES

Most reptiles spend their lives on their own, and only pair up with others during the breeding season. Males and females find one another by tracking scents, or by following mating calls.

After mating, most females lay their eggs in the soil or under vegetation. Inside the protective shell, the growing baby feeds on the egg yolk. Air can reach the baby through the shell. After a few months, the baby is ready to hatch and face the outside world. Reptile eggs take much longer to hatch than birds' eggs.

▲ Corn snakes hatch using their special 'egg tooth' to break out of the shell.

▶ Sea turtles come ashore to lay their eggs on sandy beaches. The full-grown hatchlings (babies) dig themselves out and hurry down to the sea. This newborn turtle still has the egg yolk attached to it.

Most reptiles do not look after their young after laying eggs, but crocodiles and some snakes are caring parents. Female cobras guard their eggs until they hatch out. Crocodiles, caimans and alligators look after their young hatchlings for several weeks.

▼ This Nile crocodile is washing her young after carrying them down to the water in her huge jaws.

QUICK LEARNERS

Newly hatched reptiles look a lot like their parents, only much smaller. Unlike human babies, they are able to look after themselves right from the start. We take years to grow up, but young reptiles are speedy and know to run from danger. They also know how to hunt for food.

Past and Future

The reptiles of today evolved from creatures who lived on Earth millions of years ago. At that time, there were many types of reptiles, living on land, in the sea and in the air. Dinosaurs were reptiles too.

Around 65 million years ago, the dinosaurs and many other large reptiles suddenly died out. Experts believe a giant meteorite may have crashed into Earth, raising a huge dust cloud that blotted out the sun. Earth's climate changed quickly, and food became scarce. Snakes, lizards, turtles, crocodiles and tuataras managed to survive the catastrophe, but dinosaurs and many other reptiles disappeared.

▲ Some dinosaurs, such as *Tyrannosaurus rex*, were meat-eaters. Others, like giant *Diplodocus*, were plant-eaters.

▶ One of the biggest threats to reptiles today comes from people, because they build over reptiles' natural habitats.

CHAMELEON XING

▼ The Komodo dragon, the largest lizard in the world, is now on the list of species that are in danger of dying out.

REPTILE FOSSILS

Our knowledge of dinosaurs and other reptiles that lived millions of years ago comes from fossils. These are remains such as bones, eggs and teeth that have survived because over millions of years they have turned to stone. Scientists try to piece together Earth's early history through fossils.

Today, living reptiles face many new dangers, mainly caused by humans. Around the world, people kill reptiles for their meat or skins, and kill turtles for their shells. Every day, reptiles die when cars run over them by accident. People also kill poisonous snakes out of fear. The biggest threat reptiles face is the loss of the wild places where they live. All over the world, forests, swamps, meadows and beaches are being cleared to make room for towns and farms. When their homes are destroyed, reptiles are put in danger. Now some types of reptiles are very rare, and have to be protected by law.

WEIRD-REPTILE FACTS

Anacondas

Anacondas are the world's heaviest snakes. One caught in Brazil measured over 8m long and weighed about 225 kg.

The world's smallest snakes

Thread snakes live on islands in the Caribbean.

They measure only 10 cm long and are so thin they could crawl inside a pencil if the lead were removed.

Poisonous reptiles

Small-scaled snakes from Australia are among the world's most poisonous reptiles. This snake's venom glands contain enough poison to kill 250 000 mice.

The African black mamba

This is one of the world's fastest snakes. It can slither along at speeds of up to 19 km/h over even ground.

Giant reptile

The saltwater crocodile is the world's largest reptile. It can measure over 7m long and weighs more than 1 tonne.

◀ Dwarf caimans grow about as long as a cow, 1.5m. This one is resting on a log.

Dwarf caimans

Dwarf caimans of South America are the world's smallest crocodiles. They seldom grow more than 1.5m long.

Old croc'

The oldest known crocodile lived in a zoo in Adelaide, Australia. It died at the age of 66.

Rare dragons

Komodo dragons are the world's biggest lizards, up to 3m long. These monster reptiles are found on the island of Komodo and a few other islands in Indonesia in south-east Asia.

▲ The giant Galapagos tortoise is the largest living tortoise – it can measure 1.8m from head to tail.

Record-breaking lizard

The Virgin Island gecko holds the record for the world's smallest lizard. It measures less than 3.5 cm from snout to tail-tip, but this little gecko is very rare.

Giant turtle

The leatherback is the world's largest turtle. It measures over 2m long and spends its life in the sea.

Senior tortoise

Tortoises can live to a great age. One Marion's tortoise collected from the Seychelles in the Indian Ocean was known to be at least 152 years old.

Growing pains

Many reptiles don't stop growing when they become adults. They just carry on getting bigger, so some old reptiles are giant-sized.

WEIRD-REPTILE WORDS

Camouflage
These are colours and patterns on a reptile's skin which help it to blend in with its surroundings.

Carnivore
An animal that eats mainly meat.

Cold-blooded
This describes an animal that relies on heat from the sun to warm its body. Reptiles, fish and insects are all cold-blooded animals.

Egg tooth
The hard, horny knob on a baby reptile's snout, which it uses to crack its shell when hatching.

Evolve
When an animal species changes slowly over many years, in order to suit the changing conditions in which it lives.

Extinct
When something no longer lives on Earth.

Fangs
The long, pointed teeth of some snakes, which are used to bite their prey. A snake's fangs are hollow and are used to inject poison into their prey.

Habitat
The place where a reptile lives, such as a forest or a desert.

Hatch
When a fully developed baby reptile breaks out of its egg shell.

Hatchling
A baby reptile which has recently hatched from its egg.

◀ This chameleon is enjoying a tasty snack, snapped up by its long and fast-moving tongue.

Hibernation
A deep sleep which allows reptiles that live in cool places to survive the winter cold.

Hinge
A moveable joint in the skeleton which means that a snake can stretch its jaws very wide.

Jacobson's organ
The sensitive area in the roof of a reptile's mouth, which helps it to identify smells.

Keratin
The tough, horny material from which a reptile's scales are made. Your toenails and fingernails are made of the same material.

Mammal
One of a group of animals with fur on its body, which feeds its babies on milk.

Moult
When an animal such as a reptile sheds its worn-out skin, and grows a new skin.

Predator
An animal that catches and kills other animals for food.

Prey
An animal that is hunted for food.

Scales
The thick patches of skin that cover and protect a reptile's body.

Skeleton
The bony framework that supports the bodies of animals such as reptiles, mammals, birds and fish.

Species
A particular type of animal. The Mexican beaded lizard is a species of reptile. There are about 6500 different species of reptiles in all.

▲ The stinkpot turtle is the skunk of the reptile world. It releases a disgusting smell that puts predators off attacking it.

Venom
A poisonous liquid made by some snakes, and used to kill their prey.

Vibrations
Very small movements, felt by snakes through the ground.

Warning colours
The bright colours and markings used by reptiles to warn predators that an animal is poisonous or tastes horrible.

WEIRD-REPTILE SPOTTING

Reptiles are shy creatures that mostly hide away from humans. They are quite hard to see in the wild. The best places to study them up close are zoos and wildlife centres.

Some people keep tortoises, turtles, lizards or even snakes as pets. But reptiles don't usually do well as pets. They need particular conditions and special foods to keep them fit and healthy. Many pet reptiles die because their owners don't look after them properly.

REPTILE SPOTTING

A guide to local wildlife will give details of the reptiles that live in your area or the place you are visiting. It will also tell you if there are any dangerous species. In the wild, you are most likely to spot reptiles sunning themselves in warm, sheltered places. Binoculars will help you to study reptiles from a distance, where you are less likely to scare them away.

Turtles live by streams, lakes and rivers. In some countries, you may see them sunbathing on the bank or perched on floating logs. Lizards are widespread in warm countries. They rest on sunny walls or hide under boulders. Snakes may lurk in the same places as lizards, so be very careful when you go reptile spotting. Wear strong boots, and always take an adult with you to keep you safe.

◄ A sand lizard enjoys the sun in a flower garden in Great Britain.

The best place to see reptiles up close may be your local zoo or wildlife centre. Here, reptiles are kept in conditions that are like their natural habitat. Many zoos and also conservation groups have schemes which allow you to sponsor rare reptiles and help to save them from extinction (dying out altogether). Details of some conservation groups are given below. You can also find out about sponsoring reptiles on the Internet.

CONSERVATION AND REPTILE GROUPS
World Wide Fund for Nature (WWF)
Panda House, Weyside Park,
Godalming, Surrey GU7 1XR
Website: www.worldwildlife.org

Friends of the Earth
26-28 Underwood Street,
London N1 7JQ
Tel: 020 7490 1555
Website: www.foe.co.uk

British Herpetological Society
c/o The Zoological Society of London
Regents Park, London NW1 4RY

▲ The ribbon snake lives on land and in water in North America. It is harmless.

REPTILES ON THE WEB
If you have access to the Internet, there are loads of websites you can contact to find out more about reptiles. Websites change from time to time, so don't worry if you can't find some of these sites. You can search for sites featuring your favourite reptiles using any search engine.

Reptile websites
Herp-edia, a reptile encyclopedia:
www.Webmaster@Herp-edia.com
Web of life:
www.curator.org/weboflife
WWF's endangered species page for rare reptiles:
www.worldwildlife.org/
endangered species
Animal Planet:
www.animal.discovery.com/
reptiles
BBC's natural history website:
www.bbc.co.uk/nature

INDEX

JUST FOR YOU!

Christine Leeson

Andy Ellis

LITTLE TIGER PRESS
London

Tilly Mouse opened her eyes. It was
a fresh summer morning and so early
that it was hardly light.

"Wake up," she whispered to her
brothers and sister. "It's Mum's birthday
today. We've got a present to wrap."

The other mice leaped out of bed.

"I'll help!" squealed her sister excitedly.

"No, I'll help!"

"No, me!"

Tilly stepped back
as they jostled forwards.
"Be careful!" she gasped.
"You'll break . . ."

. . . SMASH!

Too late! The present was pulled from Tilly's paws and shattered on the ground.

"Oh dear," said Tilly, looking sadly at the broken present. "Don't worry. We can still find something else before Mum wakes up. Come on, everyone."

The mice scampered outside. Overhead,
the sky was still flushed sunrise pink.
"This way," called Tilly, but her older brother
had already seen something in the shadows.

"Look! Look!" he shouted. "How about these?"

On the path was a cluster of juicy strawberries.
Tilly licked her lips. "Mmm, what a treat!"
she said. "Mum will love them."

At that moment Vole scurried out
of the dewy grass.

"Thank you," she beamed. "You've found
my strawberries. I was just taking them home
for my family's breakfast when I dropped
some. I've really got my paws full here!"

"Oh dear," said Tilly, feeling disappointed.
"We thought we'd found a present
for our mum."

"Maybe she'd like something
else instead," said Vole.
"How about those?" She nodded
towards some feathers caught
between two twigs.

"Oh, yes! They'd make a lovely downy pillow!" said Tilly, and scampered off to gather them. "Mum will be so surprised! This is going to be the best birthday present ever!"

But just then Blue Tit chirped
from above, "My feathers! Thank
goodness you've found them! I need
them to line my nest and keep my
eggs warm."

"You'd better have them back straight
away then," said Tilly. "They would
have made a lovely present for our
mum's birthday, though."

Blue Tit thought for a minute.

"Does your mum like flowers?" she asked. "I can see a nice one lying in the grass just over there."

"Oh thank you!" cried Tilly and the mice pattered off as fast as they could.

The grass was very tall and the little
mice had to push and scramble through
it to search for the flower.

"I can't see it anywhere," called Tilly.

"I can!" shouted her little brother.

"Quick, Tilly! Come here!"

He picked up a huge white
flower and waved it over
his head.

"Do you think Mum will
like it?" he asked, tottering
under the flower's weight.

"She'll love it!" said
Tilly. "It'll make a
beautiful present!
Let's hurry back
before she wakes!"

But just then a rabbit bounded over.
"Wait! Wait!" he called. "That's
my flower! My grandma's not very
well and I was taking it home for her.
I put it down and the next minute
it was gone!"

"Oh dear," sighed Tilly. "Well, then, you must take it for her. We can find another present for our mum."

"Thank you, little mice," said Rabbit as he hopped away. "I hope you find something soon."

Tilly scratched her head. The sun was
climbing above the trees into a deep blue
sky. Mother Mouse would be awake soon
and they still hadn't found a present.

Suddenly something fluttered across
the path. Tilly leaped and grabbed it . . .

. . . but it was only a piece of paper,
not nearly pretty enough for a present.

"We'll never find anything! Mum's birthday
will be ruined!" Tilly burst out.

The mice began to cry. Big tears plopped
on to the back of the paper.

"Stop!" sniffed Tilly. "We're making it
all sticky."

Then suddenly she had an idea. "Wait
here!" she squeaked. "I won't be long!"

Tilly raced off to find Vole,
Blue Tit and Rabbit. They were
all pleased to share a little of
the things they had found that
morning, and her arms were
full as she scampered back to
the other mice. They squeaked
with excitement as Tilly told
them her plan.

Soon they were all busy, shredding and
sticking, until at last the present was ready.
Tilly and the mice dashed home.

"Wake up, Mum! Happy birthday!"
they giggled. "We've got a present.
Just for you!"

Mother Mouse looked at the
picture her children had made.
It was red with strawberry, blue
with feathers and spangled
golden with pollen.

"It's beautiful!" she smiled, and
hugged the little mice close.
"Thank you, everyone. It's the
best birthday present ever!"